Hope, Healing & Happiness:
Going Inward to Transform Your Life

Copyright © 2013 by Bright Lotus Press, Angela Rose LLC

ISBN 10 148398057X
ISBN 13 9781483980577

All rights reserved. No part of this book may be reproduced or transmitted in any form or by any means without written permission from the author.

No matter where you are at this moment, you have everything you need to live the life you've always dreamt about.

—*Angela Rose*

Dedication

This book is dedicated to you. I applaud your courage for picking up this book; it is the first step in the journey to overcome any self-limiting beliefs and create a happier life in the present... and in the future.

I dedicate this book to my ninety-one-year-old grandmother, Lorraine, who is the inspirational matriarch in our family. She lives by the saying, "I can because I think I can."

This book is also dedicated to every person on this planet who has been touched by interpersonal violence or abuse. Every person knows someone who has been affected, but sadly, trauma is shrouded in shame and secrecy. After dedicating half of my life to shattering the silence of violence across the country through my work, the time has come to go beyond. The paradigm is shifting to spread the message of empowerment and hope to a broader audience.

This proverbial new chapter of my life will be devoted to helping others take control of their minds, reconnect to the love and light within, and transform into their fullest potential as human beings.

The world around us is changing rapidly, and many people feel controlled by life. It is my hope that you will find this tool useful to help you create more joy, hope, peace, and love. Simply by picking up this book, your journey inward has already begun—and for that, I honor you.

Table of Contents

Preface 2

Introduction 3

AWARENESS... 10
AFFIRMATIONS.. 18
ATTITUDE 23
ACCOUNTABILITY 29
AUTHENTICITY 33
ATTACHMENT 39
ATTRACTION 45
ACTION 48
ALTRUISM 55
ALLOWING 59

20 Tangible Tips to Empower Yourself.............. 63

Affirmations.. 64

Resources 65

Preface

As you embark on this inner journey, I want to honor your voyage and share with you my personal realization of these concepts. My emotional and spiritual awakening happened in a life-altering moment at the age of seventeen as I was bound and powerless in a stranger's car. I was kidnapped from a shopping mall at knifepoint by a man who was on parole for murder, and my entire reality shifted in this experience of feeling utterly helpless. Working to regain some sense of power, I took control over the one thing that I could: my thoughts. The perpetrator taped my eyes shut and further concealed my vision with sunglasses. He didn't know that I could see, and from the corners of my eyes I was able to consciously remember details about our route as well as identifying features of his car and his face. I thought to myself, "If I get out of this situation alive, he is NOT going to get away with this." I was extremely present in that car—I noticed every detail, every sound, every move. It was all of those memorized, catalogued details that enabled the detectives to find him and bring him to justice. It wasn't until years later—years of diving inward—that I realized the profound power of being totally mindful and aware in the present moment.

Although we can't control what happens to us in life, it is extraordinarily empowering to realize that we have the power to control our response. Life can be difficult and unpredictable. We need to learn to let go and live in the moment. When we are in the moment, we find peace. And in peace, we find joy.

Introduction

According to the National Institute of Mental Health (NIMH), anxiety disorders affect about 40 million American adults ages eighteen years and older in a given year, causing them to be filled with fearfulness and uncertainty. Moreover, studies have revealed that 1 in 4 girls and 1 in 6 boys have been sexually abused by the age of eighteen.

Groundbreaking work conducted by the Centers for Disease Control and Prevention [CDC] under the direction of my friend and colleague Dr. Vince Felitti found that approximately two-thirds of our society has been affected by one or more "Adverse Childhood Experiences" (ACE). Abuse, neglect, and emotional abandonment were included in the ACE study. As a medical doctor, Dr. Felitti's research uncovered the vast correlation between traumatic events and physical health and emotional well-being.

It is imperative that we understand our past in order to heal ourselves and create more peace and joy in our everyday lives. Throughout this book you will be led through various interactive exercises. I encourage you to write in this book and underline anything that may speak to you. Perhaps the most important piece of this journey is twofold: to be authentically truthful with your emotions, and to be kind to yourself. As we uncover hidden pieces of ourselves, we are often met with secondary emotions of shame and disappointment. I encourage you to recognize those types of emotions and then consciously release them, because they no longer serve you. You can then replace them with a thought such as *I am choosing to journey inward to create more peace and joy in my life. I am a powerful being capable of anything.*

If you have experienced some kind of abuse or abandonment in your life, I advise that you consider seeking a professional therapist who specializes in trauma. After I was abducted, I tried to be resilient and strong. I didn't want to show any signs of weakness by seeking or accepting professional help. It wasn't until nine years after the assault that I sought the help I deserved. That was when I realized that wanting to heal is a sign of strength—not weakness.

And it is critical to remember: you have to feel it to heal it.

One thing to note: this book is not intended to be religious, but there are some threads of spirituality (meaning connecting to your inner spirit) that are applicable for any type of faith.

In working to unite with your inner self, there is great power in the simple act of breathing deeply and connecting to your breath.

> **EXERCISE: The Power of Breath**
>
> *Release any tension in your shoulders and neck. Through your nose, take in a long, deep breath of clean, fresh air into your lungs, hold it for a few seconds, and then exhale out through your mouth. Repeat this ten times.*

This simple exercise is a great stress manager. It helps ground you in the space to feel more centered when you feel overwhelmed. It also helps you connect inwardly, including when issues from your youth are triggered.

I'm including the ACE questionnaire for you to fill out in order for you to openly connect to childhood trauma. In recognizing this trauma, it is a step toward releasing the pain of the past.

What's Your ACE Score?

There are ten types of childhood trauma measured in the ACE study. Five are personal: physical abuse, verbal abuse, sexual abuse, physical neglect, and emotional neglect. Five are related to other family members: a parent who's an alcoholic, a mother who's a victim of domestic violence, a family member in jail, a family member diagnosed with a mental illness, and the disappearance of a parent through divorce, death, or abandonment. Each type of trauma counts as one. So a person who's been physically abused, with one alcoholic parent and a mother who was abused, has an ACE score of three.

Prior to your 18th birthday:

1. Did a parent or other adult in the household **often or very often** ... Swear at you, insult you, put you down, or humiliate you? **or**
   Act in a way that made you afraid that you might be physically hurt? Yes or No
   If Yes, enter 1 ___
2. Did a parent or other adult in the household **often or very often** ... Push, grab, slap, or throw something at you? **or**
   Ever hit you so hard that you had marks or were injured? Yes or No
   If Yes, enter 1 ___

3. Did an adult or person at least 5 years older than you **ever** . . . Touch or fondle you or have you touch their body in a sexual way? **or**
Attempt or actually have oral, anal, or vaginal intercourse with you? Yes or No
If Yes, enter 1 _
4. Did you **often or very often** feel that . . . No one in your family loved you or thought you were important or special? **OR**
Your family didn't look out for each other, feel close to each other, or support each other? Yes or No
If Yes, enter 1 _
5. Did you **often or very often** feel that . . . You didn't have enough to eat, had to wear dirty clothes, and had no one to protect you? **or**
Your parents were too drunk or high to take care of you or take you to the doctor if you needed it? Yes or No
If Yes, enter 1 _
6. Was a biological parent **ever** lost to you through divorce, abandonment, or other reason? Yes or No
If Yes, enter 1 _
7. Was your mother or stepmother:
Often or very often pushed, grabbed, slapped, or had something thrown at her? **or**
Sometimes, often, or very often kicked, bitten, hit with a fist, or hit with something hard? **or**
Ever repeatedly hit over at least a few minutes or threatened with a gun or knife? Yes or No
If Yes, enter 1 _

8. Did you live with anyone who was a problem drinker or alcoholic, or who used street drugs? Yes or No
   If Yes, enter 1 _
9. Was a household member depressed or mentally ill, or did a household member attempt suicide? Yes or No
   ᐧIf Yes, enter 1 _
10. Did a household member go to prison? Yes or No
    If Yes, enter 1 _

Now add up your "Yes" answers: ___
This is your ACE Score.

Don't be alarmed if you have an ACE score of one or more. As mentioned, the original study found that two-thirds of the people in the study had at least one, and 87 percent of those had more than one. Many states have replicated this study with similar results. My ACE score was more than one, and I was shocked. It helped me to understand myself, and it will provide a good framework for you to embark on this journey inward. Though even if you have an ACE score of zero, you still may have childhood trauma or things in your past that are affecting your life in the present moment. Here's an example: a friend of mine took this ACE questionnaire and told me that his score was zero. Yet, he went on to say that his caregiver had been slightly emotional abusive, but it was in more of a covert way over a long period of time. Thus, even though his ACE score was zero because the trauma was veiled, he has had to work through those painful, confusing issues.

Trauma from our past can lead to over-amplified stress. Stress is defined as the body's reaction to dangerous situations—whether they're real or perceived. When you feel that you are in danger, a chemical reaction occurs that allows you to act in ways to avoid harm. According to the American Psychological Association, the part of the brain activated when this occurs is called the hypothalamus, which regulates the body's primitive, animalistic instinct that prepares the body to "fight" or "flee" from perceived attack, harm, or threat to our safety. This can manifest itself in the body through an increased pulse, quicker breathing, tightened muscles, sweat, and higher blood pressure. The first step to managing stress is to know the symptoms of stress. But recognizing stress symptoms may be harder than you think because most of us are so used to being stressed that we often don't know we are stressed until we are at the breaking point.

This state of excessive stress or hyper-arousal was necessary for our survival back in the day when mankind was being chased by sabertoothed tigers—it provided the physiological boost to prepare to either run away or attack. In our modern age, today's sabertoothed tigers can consist of an argument with a boss or partner. On a daily basis, toxic stress hormones flow into our bodies for events that pose no real threat to our physical survival. In fact, the buildup of excessive stress has been proven to threaten our physical survival, leading to disorders of our autonomic nervous system (such as headaches, irritable bowel syndrome, high blood pressure) and disorders of our hormonal and immune systems (such as chronic fatigue, depression, and autoimmune diseases like rheumatoid arthritis, lupus, and allergies.) Did you know that 60 to 90 percent of doctor visits are due to health problems related to stress?

The good news is that we have the power to consciously take steps to control and overcome stress by creating healthier routines such as meditation and exercise, and by working to change our perception of reality through cultivating a more positive inner environment. Making a mindful effort to drop inward to become aware of stressors and deliberately shift your thought process can create magic in your life. But this shift takes time and patience.

Remember to be kind to yourself during this process, and be open to your real emotions.

Now is the time to journey inward to cultivate more peace, love, and happiness.

AWARENESS

The ultimate value of life depends upon awareness and the power of contemplation rather than upon mere survival.

—Aristotle

How did you feel after taking the ACE questionnaire? Take a moment, sit quietly, and scan your emotions and thoughts. Are you feeling helpless, or are you feeling hopeful? What is your current state of mind, and what is the inner chatter saying? We all have self-talk that goes on inside our heads—but it has been there for all of our adult lives and can easily go unnoticed because it is so entrenched.

You can create more peace in your life by learning to hear the inner self-talk, staying present in the moment, recognizing that your perception can taint realty, and using the power of *awareness* to transform yourself mentally and physically.

> **EXERCISE: Listen to Your Inner Self-Talk**
>
> *Sit in a quiet place. Make sure the television, music, and external noises are eliminated. Sit, listen, and pay attention to the voice inside your head. What is it saying? What is the overall message—is it critical?*

What did your inner voice say? *What am I listening for? This is silly—I know this won't work.* When you pay attention to that voice, you might be shocked to discover how judgmental it tends to be. We can be our own worst critics. However, the great news is that we can take steps to gain ownership over that self-talk and transition it into positive talk, which I will illustrate in the affirmation section.

This section—*Awareness*—is all about staying attentive and present in each moment. Have you heard of the Japanese Tea ceremonies? All the attention is focused on the ceremonial preparation and presentation of the green tea. Each action is done with deliberate precision. The act of whisking the tea, the way in which the kettle is used, how the tea is scooped into the cup—it is all done with conscious focus.

> **EXERCISE: Stay Present in the Moment**
>
> *Make a cup of tea. Pay laser-sharp attention to every detail, and engage every sense. Take the tea bag out of the wrapper; inhale it deeply and notice the fragrance. Be intentional in every move. If your mind starts to wander and the inner talk starts to chatter, just acknowledge it with grace, let it go, and bring your attention back to the tea. Examine the teacup you are using. Smell the tea, sip it slowly, and savor the flavor. After you enjoy sipping your tea, take a walk outside and engage your senses. Be deliberate about staying in the moment. Look at the clouds; pay attention to the movement of the trees. Or if it is nighttime, study the moon.*
>
> *Stay intentional about fully engaging in the experience.*

Through this experience, you will gain a better understanding of what it is like to live in and truly *be* in the moment. Recognize the inner chatter, let it go without judgment, and turn the attention back to what you are doing.

There is incredible power and peace in staying in the moment. We can't do anything about the past, we can't control the future, so all we have is this moment. And as the saying goes . . . that is why it is called the present, because it is truly a gift. The present is the only moment we can truly control.

A Chinese proverb says, *If you are depressed you are living in the past. If you are anxious you are living in the future. If you are at peace you are living in the present.*

We have the power to stay aware and present in the moment. Yet even in the present moment, the awareness of reality can often be skewed due to our own perceptions of the world around us. As human beings, we tend to read into situations and often project our own thoughts, feelings, and fears into what other people do and say to us. This misinterpretation of what is really happening is called our lens.

Have you ever been in a situation where you heard something negative that wasn't really there? Perhaps you got defensive because you felt attacked. Later you realized what was said to you wasn't meant in the way you heard it. Or maybe you felt rejected by a friend or a partner when trying to decide on plans, but actually it was your own fear of abandonment that created this false sense of reality. These are examples of lenses.

Stacy is in her twenties and is an adult child of an alcoholic. When she was a child her father drank every night, but he was a functioning alcoholic so he never admitted to himself or his family that he had an issue with alcohol.

Her father's relationship with alcohol seemed to always take precedence over his relationship with the family. Nearly every night, as her mom and siblings sat down for dinner, there was an empty seat at the table because her dad was at the bar. As Stacy grew up, she developed abandonment issues and a lens of defensive self-protection.

Stacy has been dating Tom for years, but their relationship is getting exceedingly difficult due to poor communication. Tom has no intention of hurting Stacy, but it seems whatever he says to her, she hears it as an attack. When Tom's words are spoken, there is no malicious intent. But because Stacy felt emotionally abandoned by one of her primary caregivers as a child, she is always prepared to protect herself. For example, when Tom gives an opinion about something, Stacy doesn't engage with what he actually says; she responds with fighting words because she perceives his communication as a threat. By using the notion of awareness, Stacy is now helping their relationship by being honest with herself about her lenses and how they corrupt the perception of what was really said.

The power of awareness is being cognizant of these lenses and learning to ask yourself, "Are my lenses tainting this situation? What is really happening?" Adult children of alcoholics and those who experienced other forms of childhood trauma tend to fear abandonment or are hypersensitive or reactive because the childhood experience was often unpredictable, and the child felt powerless. Viewing the world through their childhood lenses can cause these adults to be very sensitive to triggers, which can often evoke a fight-or-flight response. Awareness is the first step to a solution.

There is a very brief moment in the space between the trigger and our reaction when we have a choice of how to react. And in that choice, there is freedom. In this process of awareness and controlling our reactions, we must be kind to ourselves. This takes practice and will not happen overnight. Think of yourself as a detective who is simply an observer of yourself, your thoughts, and your triggers.

A trigger is a stimulus in thought, word, or action that evokes a physiological response, such as a racing heart or the feeling of wanting to escalate and fight or an urge to turn around and run away. Thinking of yourself as a nonjudgmental observer who is aware of how you react after certain stimuli can help foster an understanding of the inner workings of your mind. In childhood, pathways in our brains were created, and adult children of alcoholics, abuse survivors, and those who experienced other childhood trauma can have a sensitive amygdala. This part of the brain stores memories associated with emotional events and sends impulses to the hypothalamus for the activation of the sympathetic nervous system, which mobilizes the fight-or-flight response. Meditation has been shown to help mitigate these responses.

EXERCISE: Loving-Kindness Meditation

Sit crossed-legged on the on floor or in a chair with your feet flat on the ground. Placing your hands on your legs, take three deep breaths in slowly through your nose and exhale out through your mouth. Let your heart be soft.

Let go of plans or preoccupations. Breathe gently and deeply. Think of someone in your life who has loved and truly cared for you – perhaps a parent or grandparent.

Inwardly, recite the following aimed at this person. Do this for several minutes.

May you be filled with loving-kindness.
- *May you be safe from dangers.*
- *May you be well in body and mind.*
- *May you be at ease and happy.*

Next, you will focus on yourself. This is aimed at your own well-being. Breathe gently and deeply. Inwardly, recite the following for several minutes.

- *May I be filled with loving-kindness.*
- *May I be safe from dangers.*
- *May I be well in body and mind.*
- *May I be at ease and happy.*

Breathe gently and deeply. Inwardly, recite the statements, but expand them to the community and friends, and do this for several minutes.

- *May you be filled with loving-kindness.*
- *May you be safe from dangers.*
- *May you be well in body and mind.*
- *May you be at ease and happy.*

Then finally, recite the statements directed toward someone difficult in your life, perhaps an enemy or someone who has caused you pain. Do this for several minutes.

This exercise will help you to open your heart to love yourself, your loved ones, and also the people who have harmed you. This practice of loving-kindness can help calm your mind and keep your heart open to create more peace in your life.

Being fully aware in words, tone, and body language of how you treat others (especially in interpersonal relationships) is crucial. Communication is what separates us from other life forms. The way in which we communicate with others will greatly impact our relationships—thus impacting our level of joy. The manner in which we communicate with someone was generally learned and modeled from our parents. If we didn't have a healthy example of effective communication, we have to teach ourselves so we can break the cycle. Households with abuse, an alcoholic or dysfunctional parent tends to have a lot of passive/aggressive communication.

For example, sexual abuse survivors may feel an inherent lack of control or lack of protection from their caregivers. Similarly, growing up in an environment where there was a lot of unpredictability with an alcoholic parent can send a message to children that expressing their true feelings is not safe. That adult child of an alcoholic never learned the skills to truthfully express in a safe way his or her honest emotions in a moment of anger or dislike. That child grows up and bottles his or her true feelings inside as an adult. So a common issue is emotional withdrawal or faking a happy disposition when the negative emotions are bubbling inside. With adult children of an alcoholic, there tends to be a lot of blaming others for their behavior or seeing themselves as "victims."

Accusing those we are close with for our negative feelings only takes our own power away. When your partner or coworker says something that upsets you, how do you handle it? Do you close up? Withdraw? Ignore?

Being aware of this is the first step in overcoming it—but it is very important to avoid judging yourself. In the moment when you see yourself reacting in one of those ways, take a deep breath and investigate what that feeling is rooted in; you'll usually find something from your childhood. The more aware you are, the more you can learn to understand and control your unhealthy responses.

This keen sense of awareness can cultivate not only emotional well-being but also physical well-being. This comes in the form of being aware of what we put in our bodies. Believe it or not, I completely transformed my physical body by being aware. I began to notice how often we all tend to put junk food in our mouths unconsciously in front of a television. We tend to use food to ease emotional stressors or provide comfort. So I began to ask myself, "Am I eating this to nourish my body or because it feels good?" Even if the answer was simply because it felt good, I would still eat it, but due to my acute awareness, I ate smaller amounts and enjoyed each bite more by savoring the experience.

I also made a choice to be aware of how I treated my body, so I started walking places instead of driving, and I took the stairs when I could. I would wake up and do a quick twelve-minute on-line cardio routine. I began to put a focus on this—and the results were incredible. I lost four dress sizes simply by being aware and focused. Also, I began to notice my judgments and criticisms of my body, and I began to replace this negative self-talk with affirmations of appreciation for my body.

AFFIRMATIONS

Feet, what do I need you for when I have wings to fly?

—Frida Kahlo

An *affirmation* is anything we say to ourselves in our self-talk or in our minds, whether positive or negative. Once we have the *awareness* of the self-talk, we can consciously notice when the critical voice comes in and, in that moment, release it without judgment. In that space, we willfully replace it with something positive. For example, I used to judge certain parts of my body and wished they were perfect. In that moment, I recognized the negative self-talk with a non-judgmental observation, released the thought, and replaced it with, "I cherish my body and am getting more fit and healthy everyday."

This can be done for nearly everything in your life: relationships, self-confidence, finances, fitness, health, and business success. We must be observers of our disapproving talk about ourselves, dismiss it without disparagement, and immediately replace it with something positive and in the present tense. Keeping the affirmation in the present tense is extremely important because it anchors it in your psyche. You need to say affirmations such as *I am* or *I have*.

Author Louise Hay has done extraordinary work on affirmations. I met her several years ago, and I am blown away by her grace, vitality, and joy as she approaches ninety years old. Louise is truly a pioneer in the power of the mind and its impact on the physical body. I highly recommend her book, *You Can Heal Your Life.*

When people get sick, negativity often sets in, and sometimes we get angry with our bodies or embrace the victim mode and ask, "Why me?"

There is tremendous power in noticing those types of thoughts, letting them go, and replacing them with "I accept perfect health now." This is an affirmation I learned from Louise Hay, and I have had powerful results.

> **EXERCISE: Positive Affirmations**
>
> *Take out a piece of paper and draw a line down the middle. On the left side, write down a list of at least five negative self-talk statements you have said in the past. On the column to the right, re-create each negative thought into a positive statement said in the present tense such as "I am" and "I have."*
>
> *Then take some sticky notes, write down the things you desire in life, and recite them several times a day. Examples include, "My life is filled with joy and appreciation," "I am healthy, healed, and whole," and "I love and accept myself."*

Nadia, who is in her mid-thirties, is from Pakistan. She divorced her emotionally abusive husband nearly ten years ago. This relationship left a scar on her heart because he made Nadia feel unattractive and worthless. Moreover, divorce is generally not accepted in her culture. To those around her, from the outside, she appeared radiant and happy. She has a great job at a high-end interior design firm, a huge circle of friends, and she attends a myriad of exciting international events—but she felt unhappy and unfulfilled.

Internally, she was berating herself. Nadia's inner-self talk was extremely negative; the words of her ex-husband echoed in her mind. Once she learned to recognize the negative self-talk, I taught her to immediately replace it with a positive affirmation about herself. She chose, *I am radiant and happy.* She put her affirmations in writing, and every time she heard that negative voice, she released the thought and said her personal affirmation a few times. This created an enormous shift in the joy and peace in her life.

Other examples of positive affirmations that I have seen work wonders in life concern abundance. Did you ever notice that the more stressed out you get about money, the more the money seems to fly out the window? You have the power to create abundance by shifting the focus from negative, scarcity thoughts to positive affirmations of abundance.

I started my first business in the real estate industry in my early twenties. I have been self-employed for a very long time, which enables me the freedom to pursue my nonprofit work, but that also means a paycheck is not guaranteed. I noticed that whenever I started to stress out over cash flow or let myself get into the scarcity mindset, it had a negative impact on my bottom line. But when I consciously shifted those thoughts into ones of abundance, the results were incredible.

For example, when I became aware of feelings or thoughts of lack, I immediately replaced them with an affirmation, such as *My income is constantly increasing; I am so grateful for the abundance.*

Jackie is a small business-marketing consultant who was struggling. Whenever she was about to land a contract, it seemed to disappear without warning. She was broke and fearful of not being able to pay her bills, so she fretted constantly about income—she wasn't aware of the negative talk inside her head.

Once she was conscious of those thoughts, she began to replace her scarcity thoughts with thoughts like *Wealth is pouring into my life. I am a money magnet.* After a short time of practicing this, she landed the largest contract of her career, and after a few short months, Jackie now has a cash savings of nearly $15,000.

> **EXERCISE: Affirmations for Abundance**
>
> Write down three to five affirmations for wealth and prosperity. Say these affirmations daily. Be consistent in your thoughts, words, and actions. Say the affirmations aloud before going to sleep and the first thing in the morning.
>
> Practice the affirmations with passion and energy, and truly believe them!
>
> To further reinforce this, repeat the affirmations whenever you receive money. Furthermore, practice having an attitude of gratitude when you attain anything valuable.
>
> The more grateful you are for the things you already have, the more abundance will flow into your life.

Wealth is a product of the mind—no amount of money can make you feel wealthy. It is about being grateful for what you have. Many people think, *If I could only win the lottery, then I'd be happy.* The sad reality is many lottery winners end up losing their fortunes and are broke and even unhappier than before they won. Wealth is about shifting the mind to cultivate an environment of being at peace and happy with what you have. Did you know that almost half the world—over three billion people—live on less than $2.50 a day? That certainly puts things into perspective. And what is the secret to financial freedom? It's very simple—spend less than you earn. I started my corporate career in real estate finance, and I learned firsthand how many people spent way more than they earned. My grandma always told me to pay myself first. She was from the WW II generation where saving was the norm. But in our current culture there exists a lot of materialism, greed, and one-upping thy neighbor. This is the mentality of "keeping up the Joneses."

We need to focus on abundance and investing. And where focus and energy go . . . money flows! When thinking about retirement, time is your friend with compounding interest. Many of us live in the instant gratification world where we think, "Eh, I don't need to save now. I'll worry about it when I'm older." It's human nature to procrastinate. But creating a mental attitude of gratitude, abundance, and a shift in behavior to more responsibility in dealing with finances can create miracles in your life.

ATTITUDE

The remarkable thing is, we have a choice everyday regarding the attitude we will embrace for that day.
—Charles R. Swindoll

Our *attitude* is our mental disposition at any given moment. When was the last time you had a really awful day? Go back to that day ... did everything seem to go from bad to worse? When we have a negative mental disposition, we tend to become very oversensitive and let things bother us that we'd usually just breeze over. On that really bad day, did the victim mentality set in? *Why is this happening to me? What did I do to deserve this?* Did feelings of helplessness set in? This is where the power of choice comes in—the choice to move your emotional disposition from feeling powerless to feeling powerful.

Recognizing that there are certain things we have absolutely no control of and that we need to release them does this. Whenever something out of our control arises, my grandmother and I say, "It is what it is." This attitude is also reflected in the Serenity Prayer adopted by the group Alcoholics Anonymous (AA).

Grant me the serenity to accept the things I cannot change,
The courage to change the things I can,
And the wisdom to know the difference.

Knowing the difference between what you can and cannot control, coupled with the practice of releasing the latter, creates an incredible amount of freedom.

Another aspect of this is shifting from what is wrong in your life to focusing and being thankful for what is right.

Having an attitude of gratitude will create miracles in your life.

What are you grateful for?

> **EXERCISE: Attitude of Gratitude**
>
> *Take out a sheet of paper and make a list of five things you are grateful for. Pick the one you are the most thankful for.*
>
> *Place your hands together in front of your heart, prayer style. Press your thumbs together and anchor them to your heart.*
>
> *Draw in a deep breath through your nose and release it out through your mouth. Repeat the breath three times. Say to yourself: "Thank you so much for: _____"*

Making that shift—from focusing on what is wrong to what is right—and being in a state of being grateful will undoubtedly create more peace in your life. It also helps you stay in the present moment instead of rehashing all of the negative muck from the past.

Another aspect of attitude is one of "team," instead of focusing on *I* or *me*. Try to understand the pain of others, their point of view, or their position before you try to drive your feelings home. As author Steven Covey poignantly points out in his book, *Seven Habits of Highly Effective People*, "Seek first to understand, then to be understood."

This type of mentality is a choice—the choice to try to understand others. Another choice we have is to either feel like a victim or embrace the can-do attitude. Embrace the notion that you can do it. You can make positive changes in your life. You control your own behavior and control your own thoughts, thus controlling this moment.

An inspiring example of choice is Ethan Zohn, an American professional soccer player, philanthropist, and reality television series contestant who, in 2002, won *Survivor: Africa*. With his one-million-dollar prize, Ethan co-founded Grassroot Soccer, a nonprofit organization that trains professional soccer players to teach African children about HIV/AIDS prevention. Ethan went on to launch Grassroot Soccer UNITED, an international, youth-led movement to raise money and build awareness for his foundation and mission to end HIV/AIDS in Africa. Ethan embarked on a world-record-breaking 550-mile journey on foot, from Boston to Washington, D.C . . . and he dribbled a soccer ball the entire route! Ethan has made a tremendous impact on the world, and he has inspired me for years. In 2009, Ethan was diagnosed with a rare type of cancer called CD20-positive Hodgkin's lymphoma. He kept the same positive attitude throughout treatment, including when he lost his trademark brown, curly locks due to chemotherapy. I interviewed Ethan and was moved by his attitude. He battled this cancer very publicly because he wanted to help other people.

I definitely struggled with whether I wanted to take this public because it's a very ugly and private, introspective personal time. I just didn't know if I wanted to open my life to complete strangers all over again, but I'm in a unique position to have a little bit of celebrity behind me. I thought it would be almost cathartic to use my diagnosis as a way to educate others about not only Hodgkin's but just cancer in general.

This is an opportunity for me to educate and inspire other people. That's just who I am. Ever since I was young, I've been a person who likes to make happiness real for other people. This is just another opportunity to do that. It's not the right move for everyone, I don't think, but for me it's the right thing to do. How cool is that I get to be that person, to be that face of cancer, to have the opportunity to inspire. The bottom line is I could possibly save lives by going public with this whole thing. I'm up to about twelve people now who have emailed me that "I read your article in People" *or "I saw you on TV," "I had the same exact symptoms as you were having," "I didn't know what was going on," "I went to the doctor and was diagnosed with Hodgkin's," "Without you I would have waited longer or I wouldn't have known that what was going on was potentially cancer." So that just made it worth it right there. I've been flooded with emails, Facebook, and tweets of all these people that support me—it's just overwhelming, and it makes me feel so good, and it makes me know that I'm not fighting this alone. I'm fighting it with all these other people behind me. If I can be that voice, that face of cancer, then I'm happy to do that.*

I asked Ethan, "After you've done so much for so many people, don't you get these moments of 'Why me?'"

I think things happen for a reason, and it's just a little bump in the road, and why me because this is my path in life. I've been put here on earth to inspire, educate and help people—I guess it's another little test. It'll just give me some more power and more inspiration to go out there and help others. People are "Why me, why me?" but for me, I look at it as the opposite. It's almost like a blessing because since Survivor,

I haven't stayed in one place for more than a week. I've been on the road; I've been speaking, appearances, all this stuff starting in Africa, back again, and just haven't really slowed down to enjoy what I was being lucky to experience through this whole celebrity thing. So it was kind like, "All right, you can slow down. You can reevaluate your life and find out why you're placed here and go out and do it better than before."

I definitely share the thought process that we have the ability to transform horrible things that happen to us into helping other people. I asked him, "I'm just curious, is that something you've felt since you were a kid, that you were meant to inspire other people and make a difference—or is that something that came as you were older with notoriety and fame?"

I was fourteen when my dad died of colon cancer, and before he died he told me, "Making happiness real for others is truly the greatest gift." So, since I've been fourteen, that has been my mojo. Maybe my dad said that for a reason and sent me on my path. I say to take those dark moments and use that as fuel to flip this moment around and use that so you can come out on top spiritually, emotionally, and physically.

In whatever you're going through, you're not alone. There are probably many other people that are going through similar life things . . . or worse things. Just stay positive. To use those hard times, those negative times as fuel, remain positive and use all that anger elsewhere, and turn it into something good for yourself and for others.

Even in dealing with a life-threatening situation—Ethan stayed accountable to what his dad taught him . . . to make happiness real for others. Ethan continues to inspire countless people with his attitude of grace and giving back.

ACCOUNTABILITY

It is wrong and immoral to seek to escape the consequences of one's acts.
—Mahatma Gandhi

Personal *accountability* is perhaps the most critical component to success in your personal and professional relationships. Being accountable means taking responsibility for your actions. You don't blame, defend, deflect, or deny—you hold yourself accountable for your own promises, commitments, behaviors, and actions.

I have to be open with you: I have struggled a lot with this, especially in love relationships. My ex-boyfriend Camilo, who is now a dear friend, has taught me an exorbitant amount about the importance of taking accountability. He is an incredibly sensitive and intuitive man—and has challenged me to eliminate the Three Deadly Ds: defend, deflect, and deny . . . surrounding my actions (or specifically my reactions). In his own life, he has honed the skill of being very honest about his emotions and is able to communicate his feelings very carefully. To most women, this openness of feelings would be an amazing gift—but it took me years to ascertain that, because it felt like a curse, as that type of interaction was very foreign to me.

He is very in-tune with my feelings and emotions, and he would pick up on those and soothe me if I was feeling negative or if my lenses were clouding the reality of the intentions of what was spoken. Over the years, I have cultivated a "tough guy" inner wall of strength, and it has been one of the greatest tasks in my life to let the walls come down and learn to be vulnerable with him. These walls are huge barriers to true emotional intimacy. This is where the power of accountability comes in.

Camilo has opened me to a world where two partners are open and honest about their feelings and take care of each other's emotional needs and well-being. It pains me to admit how arduous of a task this has proven to be. When I needed him, he was always there for me. If I expressed to him something I didn't like or something he said that made me uncomfortable, he was right there to make me feel better with a sincere apology, a hug, and an attitude of wanting to change whatever I didn't like to be better for me. He would naturally expect the same from me, his loving partner. Yet, my nature had been filled with justifying and making excuses for my behavior. In essence, if he communicated to me something he didn't like, I would constantly fail to own up and take accountability for myself. I would get caught up in the Three Deadly Ds: defend, deflect, deny. My lenses would perceive his open communication as an attack, and I would defend whatever action or behavior he didn't like. To add insult to injury, when he would point out that I was being defensive, I would deny it and/or deflect to focus on something I didn't like that he did.

For example, Camilo might say, "Angie, I'd like to talk to you about something that bothered me." And he would go on to carefully articulate the way he felt and what I did that upset him. Instead of apologizing, making him feel better, and moving on, I might respond by defending my action because I felt attacked. Then he might point out that he was not attacking me and that I was being defensive. Then I might say that he was being too sensitive (deny) and then I might switch the focus on how I don't like how critical he is (deflect). This is an illustration of the viscous circle of the Three Deadly Ds that avoid accountability. This often leads to an argument, which could have been mitigated had accountability been taken from the beginning.

> **EXERCISE: Accountability and the Three Deadly Ds**
>
> *Take out a piece of paper. Close your eyes and think quietly for a moment of a time that you did not take accountability for something. Maybe it was with your partner, or with a family member, colleague, or a friend. Think about a time when you demonstrated the Three Deadly Ds: defended your actions, denied your behavior, and deflected it to turn the focus to how you felt instead of the actual situation. Take a few minutes to journal about this experience, its impact, and how taking accountability might have created a different outcome.*

Accountability is also crucial in professional relationships. Are you accountable in the business world? If you don't fulfill a commitment at work, do you take accountability? Or do you blame someone else? Do you own up and admit that you did not fulfill the commitment without justification and work to remedy the situation? Or do you make excuses and fall into the victim mentality?

I used to say that I needed better time-management skills. The truth is, I can't manage time—there are only and will only be twenty-four hours in a day—but what I needed was better accountability and prioritization. This is a common problem for women, who often feel they have to live up to the superwoman syndrome. Women have been told that they have to do it all, and many moms either want to work or have to work to meet financial commitments.

Did you ever notice how the media usually shows the woman doing the household work, including cooking and cleaning? How about making the whole family accountable? When I was a child, my mom used to make a cleaning chart for household tasks, and we all would have our own roles and responsibilities; each member of the family was accountable for a tidy house.

Another aspect of accountability for both personal and professional relationships is accountability with your word—you should have integrity in everything you do and say. I've learned that I need to be accountable for embellishing to prove a point or justify a position.

For example, recently I was picking up a friend. I sent her a text to apologize that I was going to be a few minutes late. When I pulled up to her house, I called her to tell her I was outside, and the call went straight to voicemail. I wrote in another text, "I'm outside, I've called you a few times and it went right to vm." I paused; I knew I'd only called her once. I corrected the text and pressed send. I realized that I was only stretching the truth to make it seem as though I had been waiting outside longer and that I wasn't running as late as I actually was. This may seem insignificant, but I'm continuing to call myself out and correct anything embellished or not fully truthful. Personal accountability is also important when dealing with commitments to others. Being true and accountable to your word is as critical to the journey within as is being true and authentic with your own thoughts and emotions.

AUTHENTICITY

Honesty and transparency make you vulnerable.
Be honest and transparent anyway.

—Mother Teresa

To be *authentic* is to be genuine and truthful to yourself and others. Getting in tune with your own emotions can be a scary but life-altering step. My friends know me as the eternal optimist; I live my life with rose-colored glasses and always look for the best in every situation. Now to many, this would sound like a good thing, right? Well, actually it has hindered my emotional growth because I haven't always been authentic. Something bad would happen in my life, and I would run to something that made me feel good. Dancing, drinking, road trips . . . something to replace the bad feelings and make me to feel good right away.

This hampered my ability to authentically feel and get in touch with the negative feelings. In essence, I would put any negative emotions, such as feelings of sadness, rejection, or pain, into an imaginary bag and toss it over the illusive wall in my mind. All of the bags piled up, and I am continuing the journey inward to learn to process negative emotions and be authentic to myself and to others about what I'm feeling. As trite as this may sound, *you need to feel it to heal it*. Instead of running from a negative feeling, I am learning to sit with it and try to identify what the emotion is and where it might be coming from.

My emotional vocabulary used to be extremely limited (basically simply good or bad), and I went so far as to print out a list of various emotions so I could really be present and identify which emotion I was feeling.

I'm going to share a very personal example of being authentically happy and authentically honest. I was in a five-year relationship with a wonderful man with whom I was convinced I was going to spend the rest of my life. At the core, I am a hopeless romantic who loves being in love. On the surface, we seemed like the perfect couple—hopelessly in love and in the "perfect" relationship. We loved to laugh and were very affectionate with each other. My mom said that our partnership was the one that she compared all others to because we seemed so incredibly happy.

We bought a new construction, three-level townhouse in Chicago; it had soaring ceilings that opened to an upstairs loft and thirty-foot windows. Although it was over our budget, when we walked into the sun-drenched house with our realtor, it took our breath away. We made it happen—this was back in the height of the real estate market when lending was extremely lax, and we qualified for and closed on a house that we honestly couldn't afford.

There was also the financial aspect of the lack of authenticity. We seemed so secure financially on the surface, but we were piling on the debt. The dream house was way over budget and it was burying us. After we fought about something, we'd end up ignoring each other and stop communicating, sometimes for a day or more.

Even when things were really hard between us, I wouldn't tackle problems head on. I wasn't authentic. It wasn't until around our five-year anniversary that I began to reread my journals and come to the overwhelming realization that I was miserable. On the surface, I had it all: a thriving business, a great house, a wonderful relationship—but I was not happy. I had a smile painted on my face, but inside I was hurting—and I hid my pain, not just from my family and friends but also from myself.

There were serious compatibility issues in my relationship, and I was not true and authentic with what I really wanted to do with my life. At that time, I was running his business and neglecting my own dreams and desires.

I felt comfortable, I felt safe, but I wasn't fulfilled. I was longing to nurture my own dreams, but I was neglecting my authentic happiness by growing his business. Our longing is our calling, and we need to listen to it.

> **EXERCISE: Authentic Happiness**
>
> *If there were no constraints on time, money, or any other obstacle holding you back . . . what would you do? What would your life look like? What dreams or passions would you pursue? Free write in a journal about this for ten minutes.*

I ended our relationship on my birthday. When I look back on my life, I realize I have a pattern of running from relationship to relationship. I am filled with passion and get close to men too quickly. I tend to be a serial monogamist, and the concept of casual dating is very foreign to me. Years ago I wrote a song about validating myself through men and bouncing from relationship to relationship. I would be with a man for a year or two, and when things weren't going well, I'd end the relationship and move right on to the next. As I continue my journey inward, I am very authentic with myself about my patterns and the meanings behind them.

Becoming authentic with my emotions has not been easy; it is not pleasant to face the demons of the past or what you have been hiding from. However, being authentic has had a profound impact, and even my best friends have told me that they feel closer to me now because I'm being real with what I feel.

I also have been closing circles in my life by being authentic and taking responsibility. During a leadership seminar I attended, the facilitator discussed "rackets," which are persistent complaints with someone or something that leads you into a habitual way of being, thinking, feeling, or acting. These rackets aren't always rooted in truth, but rather in our version or story of the truth of what happened. We often blame external factors—especially our parents—for our struggles in life.

Growing up I gave myself the role of martyr, of the protector in the family. As the oldest child, I always felt it was my role to take care of everything and everyone—and not be authentic with my true emotions. I always had to put on a game face and try to make everything okay. This led me to bottle up my emotions and become extremely defensive in love relationships.

I am learning to control my easy-to-trigger "fight or flight" response, though it hasn't been easy. The more I am authentic with myself, and the more I allow the experience of feeling negative emotions and process them as they come up instead of running from them, the more I gain peace and control. Recognizing that it is not my fault but that it is my fight to overcome these issues has been extremely empowering.

I had the privilege of getting to know Dave Pelzer, an inspirational speaker and international best-selling author of seven books. Dave's first book, *A Child Called "It"*, was on the *New York Times Best Sellers* list for over six years. Dave's latest book, *Moving Forward*, assists people to move beyond life's trials and realize their potential is limitless. If you don't know Dave's story, he has experienced a truly extraordinary life after surviving extreme child abuse. Dave's case was identified as one of the most gruesome and extreme cases of child abuse in California's history at that time. He nearly died several times by the hands of his mentally disturbed, alcoholic mother. As a child, Dave's resilience enabled him to overcome extreme life-threatening obstacles. I met Dave when he was a keynote speaker at a red carpet event in Los Angeles for the nonprofit I founded, PAVE: Promoting Awareness, Victim Empowerment.

Dave's inspirational work has encouraged countless organizations and millions of individuals to recommit their efforts and remain steadfast to their personal convictions. In speaking with him about the intensity of his abusive past, I was amazed at his authenticity of overcoming trauma. He became in touch with his trauma in order to heal. This is an excerpt from my interview with him.

At age twelve, I weighed about sixty-eight pounds. I stuttered horribly because my mom didn't allow me to talk, and she had me swallow ammonia. I couldn't even stand up straight, and that is when the issues began. It's like being a trained animal that's been living in the basement.

My message is if you came from an abusive situation, particularly as a young child, if you can survive all that—then I

expect greatness from you! That's what my foster mom and social worker said to me.

You survived something. You survived for a reason. I'm going to say something, and I want it to resonate; I expect greatness from all of us. I expect all of us to look at the situation for what it was and not for what we think it still is. Deal with it; let it go, and become better people for it.

Part of it is you look at the situation for what it was. My mom was horrible; she was broken; she was addicted to her demons and her hatred. Yet, I have nothing but forgiveness for my mom. When I say the power of forgiveness, it's not about forgetting what happened to me. You have got to look at the perspective. You have got to slowly forgive—it sometimes takes time to do that. When you forgive, you empower yourself. It does not mean you have to forget, but it strengthens you in your resolve. Of course, it makes you a better person. It really does empower me to say, "I don't have to follow that path."

If you really want to be a success in life, you need to find things that make you happy, and you follow through. You need common sense and to follow your instincts. Most importantly, you need to have a good heart. It is not about the money, it is not about the toys: it is about the fact that you can live your life on your terms and create your own destiny.

Clint Eastwood said it best, "Get busy livin' or get busy dyin'—you decide."

ATTACHMENT

Some people come into our lives and quickly go. Some stay for a while and leave footprints on our hearts. And we are never, ever the same.

—Anonymous

As I coach some of my girlfriends on their life issues, I find that interpersonal relationships are a main concern. Finding love, keeping love, and being happy in love weigh heavily on the minds of both men and women. I have found the way to have better relationships is to love ourselves more. The more we love and care for ourselves, the happier we are, the better partners we are for those we care about, and the more people are drawn to us like magnets.

In my early twenties I enjoyed taking road trips to Colorado with my dear friend Lauren, from Madison, Wisconsin, where we went to college. There is something about the mountains and the moon that force enlightenment on inner truths. One night, we sat on the top of the Rockies with the full moon overhead floating among a sea of bright stars. The air had a crisp chill, and the fire we created provided the perfect warmth. The conversation turned to relationships, and I came to a surprising realization . . . I was almost twenty-three, and for a decade I'd had been in many long-term relationships. I had never been single in my adolescent or adult life. When times got rough, I would break up with a boyfriend, and I always had someone waiting in the wings. I went from love to love to love—but I was lost. I didn't really know myself, and I made the hard discovery that I didn't really love myself either.

That realization was a bitter pill to swallow. I sought love to fill a void; what I really needed was the love and approval of the most important person in my life . . . me.

At that point in my life, I was living with a man I had been dating for several years. When I returned home from Colorado, I told him that I didn't want to re-sign our lease. I explained that I still wanted to be with him, but in order to be a better partner for him, I needed to live on my own. He didn't understand or appreciate that—and so our relationship ended, and I was on my own for the first time.

I was unattached, excited to experience life on my own terms, and looking forward to going inward and learning to love and appreciate myself.

So how did I do this? I began to date myself. I bought myself flowers, I went on road trips alone, I went camping alone—I became very empowered by my solo adventures. (I don't recommend this from a safety perspective—I slept with a butcher knife under my pillow when I camped alone.) I had a good group of friends, but some nights I went to see live music alone. I journaled constantly and was learning to appreciate myself. During this time, I also began to think about my perfect life partner. I made a list of the traits I was looking for. No one is perfect, but I think knowing the one or two non-negotiables is critical.

EXERCISE: Know Your Non-Negotiables

Make a list of the character traits of your perfect partner. Even if you are already in a relationship, set your partner's traits aside. Now ask yourself to define the ten to fifteen characteristics that are important to you in a mate. Then look at the list and circle one or two things that are "must-haves." These are your non-negotiables.

It is important to know your non-negotiables in relationships. If you have a partner who doesn't possess your non-negotiables, it can be exceedingly difficult to make a relationship work. Let me be clear, though: if a potential mate is willing to work to acquire the non-negotiables you seek, don't rule that person out. My personal non-negotiable is to have a partner who really sees and appreciates me, who "gets" me. I have felt very misunderstood for a lot of my life, and being appreciated and understood are monumental. In my mind, this meant appreciation for all of my positive traits—but over time, I've learned that it also includes having a partner who understands my weaknesses and helps me overcome them.

What does a healthy relationship look like?
Here are some signs of a healthy relationship:
- ❖ Supportive
- ❖ Respectful of oneself and each other
- ❖ Good communication
- ❖ Equality
- ❖ True comfort in being your true self
- ❖ Strong friendship
- ❖ Sense of interdependence

What does an unhealthy relationship look like?
Here are some sample signs of an unhealthy relationship:
- ❖ Jealousy and distrust
- ❖ Codependence
- ❖ Fear
- ❖ Lack of support for things you enjoy
- ❖ Manipulation

- ❖ Selfishness
- ❖ Guilt for spending time with friends and family
- ❖ Forced sexual contact
- ❖ Threat of violence

Even if there is no physical violence in your relationship, emotional abuse can be just as traumatic. My friends who have endured emotional abuse (such as their partners berating them or making them feel like they are worthless) describe emotional abuse as a wound on your soul, and the invisible scars from this damage can last an extremely long time.

If you are in an unhealthy or abusive relationship, you can reach the National Domestic Violence Hotline at thehotline.org. or call 1.800.799.SAFE (7233).

We often attract partners who mirror what we experienced at home as we grew up. We need to be aware and recognize the kind of partners we attach ourselves to—and if those relationships are not healthy, we need to be intentional about changing our selection process.

EXERCISE: You Attract What You Know

On a sheet of paper, draw two large circles side by side. Above the circle on the right, write the name of the first caregiver in your life (typically a mother or father), and above the second circle, write the name of a second caregiver. (If you come from a single parent household, perhaps it is a grandparent.) Then list all of the traits (both positive and negative) of those caregivers. Be open and thoughtful. Then, circle the couple of traits that most impacted your life (positive or negative). Now, see if your partner (or if you are single, the type of partner you tend to attract) possesses one or more of these. And if those traits are unhealthy or don't serve you, you can purposefully change what you attract.

For example, Libby, who is fresh out of college and has bright eyes and a big smile, has always attracted partners who liked to party with excessive drinking. She admits that she, too, used to deal with every emotion—happiness and celebrations or sadness and desperation—with a vodka tonic or beer and a shot of whisky. When she became conscious of that, she deliberately decided to live her life in a healthy way. And in this purposeful move, she knew what she wanted to attract: She wanted someone who took good care of his body, someone who she could workout with, someone who didn't need to get smashed every weekend to enjoy life and have fun. She took the action to become a better "her" to attract a healthy partner with whom she could share her life and raise a family in a healthy way.

If we want to have better quality relationships, we need to be the best partners we can be. We humans tend to have double standards in relationships—sometimes we expect to be treated a certain way without providing that same treatment to our significant others. If we are in a relationship that is struggling, we need to take a look at our role in it.

It's also powerful to understand that every person gives and receives love differently. Gary Chapman, PhD, the author of the *New York Times* bestselling book *The 5 Love Languages,* breaks down the five ways in which people show love: Words of Affirmation, Acts of Service, Affection, Quality Time, and Gifts. He discusses that we often give love in the way in which we want to receive it. This can be problematic if our love language is not the same as our partners'. In order to have a better relationship, we need to be a better partner—and be committed to loving ourselves throughout the process.

ATTRACTION

Let a person radically alter his thoughts, and he will be astonished at the rapid transformation it will effect in the material conditions of his life.

—Napoleon Hill

For over a century, the concept of the "Law of Attraction" has permeated the self-help movement and has inspired countless books on the topic. The basic notion is that we *attract* what we think. If we think negative thoughts, we attract negative circumstances. If we think positively, we will attract positive circumstances. There have been many scientific tests that illustrate the difficulty of proving this with any precise, measureable results. This is, in part, because it is incredibly subjective. That being said, I have used Law of Attraction principles to manifest many joyful experiences in my life.

The principle of attracting what you desire is to first *know* what it is you want and *believe* you can attain it. Once you know what you want, you should cultivate positive emotions about it. Feel the joy of obtaining what you desire. Then, you need to take time to imagine what it will be like by closing your eyes and imagining yourself in that moment. Make time to daydream, to wish, to ensure that what you think in a positive way matches positive emotions.

In my life, I have seen this work several times. When I was fresh out of college, I got a corporate job working in real-estate finance. The corporate headquarters came out with a contest and the grand prize was an all-expense-paid trip to Hawaii. Let me be clear: I was not the top producer in my office, let alone in the region or in the country. My sales numbers were pretty good, and I had great customer service, but there was no way I was going to win this trip. But I *really* wanted it. I felt a tingle in my chest and a blast of bliss whenever I thought about it. Using the Law of Attraction each night before I went to bed, I would picture myself on the beach and imagine what it would feel like. My partner and I would think about what it was going to feel like to lie in the sand, feeling the sun on our faces, looking at the palm trees as we felt the tropical breeze. Weeks later came the big announcement about the winners of the trip.

"*For the first time ever, instead of just using the numbers of those who had the most sales, we are incorporating the customer service scores into the decision.*"

Due to my nearly perfect customer service rating—and leveraging attraction—I won an all-expenses paid, seven-day trip to Hawaii! They also gave me $1,000 in spending money!

I continued to use this visualization for the rest of that year. *Sitting on the beach, what it's going to feel like, how is it going to be?* And soon after, I was booked for a multi-day educational initiative in the Bahamas. The event organizers created a welcoming reception at the United States Embassy. It was extraordinary! I was so incredibly grateful. And that feeds into the Law of Attraction—when you receive something you have been dreaming of, make sure you take time to be thankful!

And also, don't sweat the details. You can know what you want, but the path to getting there might not be exactly what you expected. But you have to believe that everything is working out for your highest good. Know what that goal is, but be a little fluid and realize that you might not get there in the exact route you expected.

EXERCISE: The Power of Visualization

Think of something that you really want, and write it down. Each night for two weeks, take ten to fifteen minutes envisioning yourself when you receive it. Feel the joy of your desire. Focus on engaging all of the senses. What does it feel like? What does it look like? What does it smell like? Concentrate on the blissful feeling in your heart. During the day, inwardly focus on that feeling of the desire! Don't doubt the process—know and trust that your needs are being met.

If you don't receive exactly what you want, don't get discouraged. Try it again, and be aware of your negative self talk. If it creeps in, remember to acknowledge it without blaming or judging yourself. Let it go and replace it with a positive affirmation, and keep the cycle of positive thinking with fostering cheerful emotions.

There are a myriad of so-called "self-help" books that stress the power of positive thinking and visualization as the sole source of achieving what you desire. While I accept that these things are indeed important, you can't *only* think your way to success—you need to take action!

ACTION

What you do is what matters, not what you think or say or plan.
—Jason Fried

Action is at the root of creating what you desire and having more joy in life. You have to know what you want and take the action to get it. Of course you must begin with visualizing the end result (that is critical), but action must be taken to get there.

Since college, I've been saying that my recipe for action has been *PDP: Passion, Drive, Persistence*. You must have the *passion* to achieve something, plus the *drive* (motivation) to make it happen, plus the *persistence* to not give up even when you are facing failure. For example, I founded a national nonprofit, PAVE: Promoting Awareness, Victim Empowerment. I created PAVE to shatter the silence of sexual violence as a student organization when I was in college, but I always had a vision of it growing to be a national group.

I had the passion for it because I experienced first-hand how difficult sexual assault can be to endure; I had the drive and motivation to keep it going for over a decade and the persistence to continue even when things seemed impossible. In times where it was extremely difficult to balance everything because it wasn't my full-time job, but I never gave up . . . though honestly, sometimes I thought about it.

When you put these three qualities together into play in your life, there's no telling what you might accomplish!

EXERCISE: PDP: Passion, Drive, Persistence

What is one tangible goal that you would like to achieve? Create a goal that is SMART, which stands for Specific, Measurable, Attainable, Relevant, and Timely. (SMART is a key concept in project management.) Then answer these questions:

- Why are you passionate about this goal?
- What will keep you motivated and driven to complete this?
- What are some tools you will put in place to persist, even when you feel like giving up?
- How can you ensure success?

One of the hardest lessons I learned along the way was not taking just any action, but using the power of saying no in order to hone in on a specific goal.

Looking back, I wore so many hats in college that it was really ridiculous. I was a full-time college student at the University of Wisconsin-Madison; I managed a photography company, founded and directed PAVE, founded and directed MOSA: Men Opposing Sexual Assault, served as the Women's Issues Diversity liaison through the student government, and was elected as the state president of the Wisconsin Chapter of NOW: National Organization for Women. Wow—just typing that list gave me a little ping of anxiety. I constantly felt like I could barely keep my head above water. I was physically sick much of my collegiate career with a recurring throat and chest virus. Now, I understand why. My physical body and its state of health (or illness) was in direct relation to my mental health. It was a mirror. Whenever I felt like I was drowning, I would get sick. Why did I take on so much?

Because I felt like I had to say *yes* to everything I was asked to do; I thought every opportunity was a gift. Now I realize the power in being able to say no to things in order to focus on the most important goals.

If you are a high achiever, one important tip is to find coaches and mentors. For whatever you want to do, for any dream that you want to make into reality, it is very important to find someone who has done it and to learn from them. There is no need to reinvent the wheel: take advice from people who have done what you want to do . . . and then do it better with your own spin!

We all want to make a difference in the world . . . and *you* matter. What you are passionate about matters. What you want to do or what you want to change matters. And you have no idea the power in one person's voice. I founded PAVE because of all the people who disclosed to me that they had been affected by violence; I saw an ill in the world and wanted to change it. I saw the power of simply using your voice and taking action, and now we have nearly fifty chapters and affiliates across the country.

One major hindrance to action is what I call parking in the *Procrastination Station*. For example, can you remember a time when you were being productive, maybe studying or working, and then you opened Facebook. You think, *Hmm, I wonder what my friends are up to. I'll just be on for a second.* Those seconds turn into minutes, and pretty soon, *Whaaaat? I've spent an hour and a half on Facebook?* We need to be very mindful of where our time goes. We can easily get parked in the Procrastination Station. I started keeping a record of exactly where I'm spending my time.

> **EXERCISE: Time Flies**
>
> Keep a calendar (physical or online) and mark down where all of your time is spent for a week, including your work time, free time (including Facebook, YouTube, Twitter, Pinterest, and other social media), and time with friends. Then print out a copy and make groupings that make sense, such as Schoolwork, Client Meetings, Social Media, Family Time, or others that are general categories for your life. The importance lies in being authentic and specific during the exercise: If you spent an hour on Facebook at work, mark it down! Assign each category a color, and then use crayons, colored pencils, or markers to color each entry and see where you spend time. Is this what you want your calendar to look like? Do you need to change something around and prioritize your time?

Being organized and efficient is another impactful action step. Do you struggle with organization? I certainly did. As a kid, my room would always have an explosion of clothes on the floor, and it didn't bother me. Now, I do not feel comfortable in a disorganized environment. Your physical space is a reflection of your inner space. If you are disorganized in your home, you likely feel disorganized internally. It makes a world of difference to create systems to stay organized. You can even hire an organization consultant to help you get organized. You don't have to have a strong suit in organization; the important thing is that you find a way to create a living environment that creates a feeling of peace and zen.

Knowing your strengths is also an important aspect of action at home and at the office or school. We are not good at everything, so play to your strengths! Embracing your strengths and weaknesses creates an incredible freedom. An example in my life is with PAVE. My weakness is that I don't like being behind a desk all day. My strength is meeting and engaging with people. So the action I'm taking is to foster the "busy work" temporarily so later I can pass the torch. I need to create efficient processes for the nonprofit so I can delegate to other people. But it doesn't come without hard work and being methodical about the creation of the end result.

Another aspect of action with organization and efficiency is getting rid of "stuff." When I moved from Chicago to Washington, DC, I got rid of half of my belongings, and it felt so freeing. There is only so much you can do when you are bogged down with so much stuff! Make a habit of purging your clothes and donating them to a local charity.

While all of these are important steps, I want to share one of the greatest real-life examples of using action—a young man named Clay Treska.

Marine Staff Sergeant Clayton Treska transformed his life and used action to defy all odds—including death. I first met Clay at a party years ago; his sister Julie was a friend and colleague. His broad shoulders and chiseled jawbone commanded every woman's attention. But what struck me about Clay was the juxtaposition between his rock-hard physique and his soft, gentle nature. He was very easy to talk to. Clay was stationed at Camp Pendleton in San Diego, and he was sent overseas on a private mission with an elite squad of the Marines.

After facing death in the line of combat, Clay was forced to face another killer upon his homecoming from overseas—cancer. Shortly after returning from his tour in Iraq, he was diagnosed with testicular cancer. He fought the cancer hard, and it went into remission.

One of his life-long dreams was to compete in the Ironman Triathlon, which is a series of long-distance triathlon races consisting of a 2.4-mile swim, a 112-mile bicycle ride, and a 26.2-mile run, raced in that order and without a break. This grueling race can cause some of the most well-trained and healthy athletes to fall. But not Clay.

He continued to prepare for the Ironman, but while he was training, he started to experience severe back pain. He went back to the doctor and he was given a pernicious prognosis—the cancer was back with a vengeance. At age thirty, Clay was diagnosed with Stage IV terminal cancer. He was given mere months to live. But this did not deter Clay; he vowed to fight and took action to overcome certain death.

Even as the doctors wanted to prepare Clay for hospice care, he insisted he was not only going to fight the cancer but simultaneously train for Ironman. In the hospital, he endured chemotherapy and brutal stem-cell treatment. As his body increasingly deteriorated, Clay clocked the laps around the nurse's station with his IV bag, did yoga, sit-ups, and meditated when the pain was too great.

While he was still in the hospital, he astonished everyone by competing in the Half Ironman. Clay went on to later compete in the full Ironman competition, and he is now cancer-free. Clay took action to beat all odds, and even when the prognosis was deadly, he never gave up. If Clay can conquer Stage IV terminal cancer, you can conquer any obstacle in your life.

ALTRUISM

There is no exercise better for the heart than reaching down and lifting people up.

—John Holmes

The definition of *altruism* is the unselfish regard for or devotion to the welfare of others. Essentially, it's the way in which you spread love and light into the world. Perhaps this is through volunteering for a local nonprofit, raising donations for a cause, or maybe through the way in which you treat everyone around you—in an altruistic, selfless, and giving manner.

We all have a social ill we would like to see fixed. What is yours? What are you passionate about?

EXERCISE: Activate Your Altruism

The exercise for this section is to find a way to give back—and schedule it. Perhaps it will be for you to clean out your closet... do you have suits or dress clothes you can donate to the organization Dress for Success, which provides interview dress suits, confidence boosts, and career development to low-income women? Can you create a food drive at work for a local food bank? Can you volunteer at Meals On Wheels?

As I was traveling the country and talking about the subject of altruism, I realized that although I was volunteering for my nonprofit PAVE, I wasn't really giving back in my own neighborhood. The neighborhood where we bought our townhouse in Chicago was Humboldt Park—a traditionally low-income and gang-infested community that was undergoing gentrification. There was a middle school two blocks from my house, and that was where I decided I wanted to give back. As school budgets continue to get cut, so do the art, music, and theatre programs. Since I had a theatre background, I thought that would be a great way to give back to these eleven- and twelve-year-old students. So I met with the principal and created an after-school theatre program. I picked some monologues and was shocked to find that many of these kids had a very hard time reading. So I decided to allow them to create their own monologues that spoke to their lives—they could create anything they wanted. It was so exciting to see the range of topics: everything from the love they had for their grandmas to the pain of loosing a loved one to gang violence. We invited all of the parents, friends, teachers, and loved ones to the performances, and I was so honored to be a part of that creative process. The talent was incredible, but even more incredible was the shift in their levels of confidence and the impact on their self-esteem. Those students walked taller, spoke louder, and held themselves with more confidence afterward.

    I also volunteered with an after-school mosaic mural program created by my friend Kamelia. She created the organization Green Star Movement, which is a nonprofit in Chicago that empowers individuals, brings communities together, and beautifies the public space with giant mosaic murals. There is a lot of power in making time for creativity—and doing that while giving back can be extremely rewarding.

    It can also be beneficial to take some aspect of pain in your life and transform it for the good of others. One personal example is PAVE's *The Binding Project*, which I helped create. When I was abducted from a shopping mall, the perpetrator used plastic zip ties to bind my hands behind my back. I felt completely helpless—like a captured animal. Those zip ties were the one thing that would trigger me: I would see them in a store, and it would bring me back to that day of feeling totally powerless. One day I was shopping with a friend, and we were debating ways to acknowledge the anniversary of that fateful day when I saw zip ties on display. I stood there and stared at them blankly, my face as white as a sheet. My friend saw my reaction and asked what caused it. After I explained to her how painful my experience was, she exclaimed, "Angela, that's it! You need to own those!" And so was born *The Binding Project*, an international art empowerment campaign where participants write a word of empowerment on two plastic zip ties—one that they wear to show solidarity with the movement and one they submit to us to be included in an installation art piece. Some groups use *The Binding Project* to raise donations for PAVE. I have been so surprised to see how many college fraternity men and male athletes have supported this project! It's important to see men and women working together to end violence.

This project has helped other people connect to their triggers and take ownership over them. Ashley Dunn was raped by her OB-GYN on Valentine's Day. What do you think triggered her? Hearts. Valentine's Day Cards. Things that traditionally represent love and joy became a source of pain for Ashley.

Inspired by *The Binding Project*, Ashley created a rally where hundreds of people rallied at the Texas state Capital and marched with giant Valentines and hearts to raise awareness about sexual assault. Ashley worked to reclaim Valentine's Day and now celebrates happily with her loving husband. Her work has impacted others dealing with issues of trauma, and so goes the power of paying it forward. If we all make an effort to spread a little love and light everyday, the world will be an even better place to life.

ALLOWING

Love yourself first, and everything else falls in line. You really have to love yourself to get anything done in this world.

—Lucille Ball

There are many aspects to the term *allowing*. It means making time to connect back to yourself through self-care and creativity; it means creating the ability for everything you desire to flow into your life without self-sabotage; it means acceptance by releasing judgment of others and ourselves.

We move so fast through life—rushing to work, rushing to meetings, rushing home, rushing, rushing, and then sitting down in front of the television in the evening to turn off the noise from the day. But the television is not allowing us to connect back to ourselves—we need to make time for that. This can be done through hiking a local trail, going for a long walk on a beach, watching the sunset—taking in all of the beauty of nature, remembering to breath deeply, and feeling the peace within. I am very passionate about extreme self-care, because the more you take care of yourself, the better you can take care of the people you care about and all other aspects of your life. It can be very difficult, especially for women, to take time for ourselves. What we need to remember is that it doesn't have to be long or expensive—even a fifteen-minute foot or shoulder massage can bring so much joy and peace.

I was speaking at an international conference and had been running around giving many workshops. I was feeling stressed and had very low energy. I decided it was time for some self-care, so I found a local spa and treated myself to a fifteen-minute chair massage, which was only fifteen dollars, and it completely changed my day. I was filled with peace, love, focus, and gratitude. Give yourself permission for self-care, and make time for it.

Another way to connect to our inner selves is through creativity. Everyone is inherently creative, even if you don't consider yourself an artist. There are many ways you can cultivate creativity, alone or in a group setting, through drawing, painting, sculpting, pottery, collage making, or music. You can also be creative in cooking or creating gifts for friends.

After college, I lived in a hip Chicago neighborhood with my friend Missy. We had Creative Night soirees where we bought a large canvas, painting supplies, wine, and invited a group of friends. Throughout the night when someone felt inspired, they would add to the collective art piece. We stifle ourselves if we use the excuse that we are not artistic, because every human being is inherently creative, and we need to make the time to allow it.

EXERCISE: Create a Vision Board

A vision board is a collage of images and affirmations of your dreams and desires. A vision board is simply a visual representation of the things you want to have, be, or do in your life. It is thought to help to attract the things into your life that you desire.

- *Decide the main theme of your board. It may be based on something specific you wish to accomplish or obtain, or it may be a general idea of everything that makes you happy.*
- *Gather various types of magazines—including outdoor, sports, fashion, and other genres.*

> - *Find pictures that correspond with your theme, either from these magazines or from photographs and/or images from the Internet.*
> - *Print (if necessary) and cut out your pictures. You can also type or write some affirmations that correspond with your theme.*
> - *Glue your pictures and affirmations to your poster board.*
> - *Hang your vision board in a place you will see every day.*
> - *View your board at least once a day, and focus on the objects, sayings, and theme of your board.*

Another aspect of allowing is accepting good to flow into your life without self-sabotaging. If the inner voice is talking negatively, it has the ability to undermine the flow of your desires into your life. My dear friend Tanya has taught me so much about the notion of self-actualization, which is the process of transforming into your best and highest self. You need to allow the core of who you are to fully embrace believing in yourself. Grow self-confidence, which builds self-esteem. You need to believe that you deserve only good things and that you deserve to live a joyful life filled with bliss and peace. You need to accept and allow this into your life and commit to it. Make a commitment to yourself to continue to master your thoughts and release self-limiting beliefs.

You are worth it, and you can do anything. You are all-powerful, and you can do this. Your past does not define you. Everything that happened yesterday doesn't matter—it is this moment that matters. Allow yourself to be fully present in this moment. Forgive yourself. Love yourself. Allow the love, joy, and abundance to flow into your life. Accept yourself for who you are, and release the judgment of yourself and others. When you hear the critical inner voice, simply acknowledge it with a smile and release it. Those limiting beliefs no longer serve you. Replace it with an affirmation such as *I allow joy, peace, and abundance to flow into my life. I am so grateful.*

You are embracing your higher self—the inner light that may have been covered over in onion layers of trauma. Allow the onion layers to be peeled back and let your light shine; your soul has always been whole. Break the cycle. There are many books on topics like the ones we've touched on here—allow yourself to continue this journey.

Allow yourself to reconnect to the child inside you. Be playful, even for a few short moments. Dance in your living room. Skip down a street. Be silly. Be free. Let go. Do you feel like your life will be over if you just stop? Breathe. This moment is *the* moment. The journey *is* the destination.

Healing old wounds by living in peace and joy is possible, but you have to make the choice to regain control of your mind, body, and soul. Get your power back. Be joyful, be loving to yourself. Remember, you are whole. You are an extraordinary human being, so act as if you know are, even if you have some level of doubt or fear. Allow yourself to release the fear, allow yourself to release the doubt. Accept yourself wholly with love and without judgment.

Commit to a path of continuous improvement for the mind, body, and soul. Treat yourself and others with love. Make the choice to live in the light.

No matter where you are at this moment, you have *everything you need* to live the life you've always dreamt about.

20 Tangible Tips to Empower Yourself

1. Take a brisk walk, breathe deeply, and appreciate the beauty of nature. Be in the present moment.
2. Picture yourself where you want to be in five years. Write a note from your future self to your present self—what do you want yourself to know?
3. Realize that your life is fluid and nothing is set in stone—you can change your path at any time. You are free from the constraints of your past.
4. Keep a journal—free-write without over thinking.
5. Invite friends over for a vision-board-making party.
6. Volunteer at a local nonprofit.
7. Do a random act of kindness for a stranger.
8. Write down five things you appreciate about yourself.
9. Do ten minutes of yoga every morning; I personally like Sadie Nardini's YouTube channel.
10. Say you are sorry more often and seek to understand your loved ones.
11. Look at yourself in the mirror and say, "I Love You."
12. Turn off the TV and read a book about creating your best self.
13. Take time to close your eyes to daydream about something you desire.
14. Take time to do something for yourself. Even when things are very busy, treat yourself to a fifteen-minute shoulder or foot massage.
15. Take time to be creative, such as coloring, drawing, painting, sewing, or creating pottery.
16. Find a YouTube guided meditation.
17. Remember that your soul is whole, even when you feel broken. Say to yourself, "I deserve to love and be loved."
18. Be gentle to yourself. When you hear your inner voice being critical, don't judge—just let it go, and replace it with a positive affirmation.
19. Breathe in deeply and connect to this very moment.
20. Know that you are not defined by your past, and, at any moment, you can change the trajectory of your life by taking control of your mind.

Sample List of Affirmations

There are countless affirmations that you can use, but here are a few examples to get you started.

WEALTH
I am so grateful for the abundance in my life.
My income is always increasing.
All my needs are met, and I am thankful.

RELATIONSHIPS
I attract only healthy relationships into my life.
I deserve to love and be loved.
I live with an open heart and allow love to flow into my life.

HEALING
I choose to forgive those who have harmed me.
I am breaking the cycle of dysfunction and choose to heal.
I feel whole and give myself permission to be happy.
I allow myself to embrace the child within.

HAPPINESS
I am in the present moment and in a state of calm and peace.
I radiate joy, and I am grateful for the gifts in my life.
I am making positive changes in my life, and I am happy.
I allow myself to be creative.

HEALTH
I love and appreciate my body.
I honor my body and am becoming more fit every day.
I choose to make positive, healthy choices for myself.
I accept ideal health now.
I am living a healthy life and my body reflects this.

SUCCESS
I follow my dreams and honor my purpose.
I choose to live a balanced life.
I believe in myself and in all my unique talents.
I forgive myself for not being perfect, and I know that I am a powerful being capable of anything!

Resources

Benson Henry Institute for Mind Body Medicine
www.massgeneral.org/bhi/
1.617.643.6090

National Domestic Violence Hotline
www.thehotline.org
1.800.799.SAFE (7233)

The National Suicide Prevention Lifeline
www.suicidepreventionlifeline.org
1.800.273.TALK (8255)

The National Eating Disorders Association (NEDA)
www.nationaleatingdisorders.org
1.800.931.2237

National Sexual Assault Hotline
https://ohl.rainn.org/online/
1.800.656.HOPE

PAVE: Promoting Awareness, Victim Empowerment
www.ShatteringTheSilence.org

Alcoholics Anonymous
www.aa.org

Hay House Books—Louise Hay
www.HayHouse.com

Adverse Childhood Experiences (ACE Study)
www.acestudy.org

Imerman Angels—Cancer Support
www.imermanangels.org

Thank you for your commitment to journey inward. Please stay in touch with me!

Tweet me: @AngelaRosePAVE, or share your thoughts and be in touch with me on my Facebook page: http://facebook.com/AngelaRoseInfo

Website: www.AngelaRosePave.com

A special thanks to Simon Weinberg for encouraging me to write this book and to Vincent J. Felitti, MD, for use of the ACE study. A giant thank-you to my dear friend and editor Candace Johnson, who never stopped believing in me. A heartfelt thanks to Camilo, Lorraine, Missy, Tanya, Kamelia, Lauren, Gina, Cara, Susan, Frank, Autumn, Linda, Kristin, Kristen, Carter, Lilia, Sumrien, and the PAVE family. Photo credit to Jodi. Special thanks to Tim Samp for graphic design.

Made in the USA
San Bernardino, CA
29 July 2017